T0094821

ADVENTURES FOR BORED ADULTS

ADVENTURES FOR BORED ADULTS:

GAMES. CHALLENGES. ACTIVITIES. TREATS.

Paula McGuire

POP PRESS

Pop Press, an imprint of Ebury Publishing,
20 Vauxhall Bridge Road,
London, SW1V 2SA

Pop Press is part of the Penguin Random House group of companies
whose addresses can be found at global.penguinrandomhouse.com

First published by Pop Press in 2021

www.penguin.co.uk

A CIP catalogue record for this book is available from the British Library

ISBN: 9781529148602

Printed and bound in Great Britain by Clays Ltd, Elcograf S.p.A.

The authorised representative in the EEA is Penguin Random House Ireland,
Morrison Chambers, 32 Nassau Street, Dublin D02 YH68.

Penguin Random House is committed to a sustainable future
for our business, our readers and our planet. This book is made
from Forest Stewardship Council® certified paper.

CONTENTS

CHALLENGES 39

INTRODUCTION

They say that only boring people are ever bored. They're wrong.

Boredom is a universal enemy, waiting to strike behind every bad film choice and rainy Sunday afternoon, and if you don't know how to access the antidote, it can poison your entire outlook on life. Thankfully, adventure exists to save us all from the ravages of boredom, and once you start noticing adventure, you'll spot it everywhere you go.

The key to finding adventure is knowing where to look for it. Or, more accurately, where not to look. It's not hiding on the other side of the world from you; neither is it lurking somewhere beyond your next pay rise. Adventure doesn't play hard to get.

After spending a year trying something new every day, it became abundantly clear that never in a million lifetimes would I run out of different things to try, and that's because, almost immediately, I started to bring the spirit of adventure to even the most mundane parts of my day. And that's the real secret: adventure isn't out there, it's inside, just waiting for you to apply its magic to your world.

Whether you're spending time at home or venturing outdoors, on your own or entertaining friends, *Adventures for Bored Adults* was written for every situation – from hen or stag dos to staycations, get-togethers and self-care days – and it will give you something fun and easy to do without the interference of a screen. Play a new game, take up a challenge, try a fun activity or just allow yourself a special treat; whatever your mood, there's an adventure for you.

All you have to do is turn the page.

HOW TO USE THIS BOOK

ADVENTURERS	LOCATION	DIFFICULTY
🧍	🏠 🚶	👍

Throughout the book, look out for 'adventurers' 🧍 for the amount of participants, 'at home' 🏠 or 'on the move' 🚶 symbol, and the 'thumbs up' symbol 👍 for level of difficulty (the games get more complicated as you go through the text).

You might wish to use some of the games and challenges as drinking games – if so, make up your own rules and act responsibly.

Some games carry a warning: ⚠ PLEASE ADVENTURE RESPONSIBLY!

GAMES

Games: whether they are strict or silly, traditional or completely made-up, what they all have in common is that they can turn even a boring old truth into entertainment with just a little dare. A game can test your skills, your memory or your patience. You can play on your own, with family and friends or with complete strangers – even if they don't realise they're playing.

When there doesn't seem to be much fun in the world, you just have to make some of your own. And games are a pretty good place to start.

Solo Games

YES!

ADVENTURERS	LOCATION	DIFFICULTY
👤	🏠 🚶	👍

Yes! is the simplest game you can imagine, as there's only one rule: you have to agree to everything for an entire day. Will you take the dog out? Yes. Can I borrow a tenner? Yes. Will you lend me your car for a bank job. Ye . . . Actually, I think I'll let you make your own judgement on that one. Don't tell anyone that you're playing the game (or you might find your new willingness being abused), and keep it going for as long as you can without getting yourself into any compromising positions.

PERFECT FOR: entertaining yourself quietly, figuring out your limits.

SECRET RACES

ADVENTURERS	LOCATION	DIFFICULTY
🧍	🚶	👍

Not all games need formal rules or points systems – or even for players to know they're actually playing. For Secret Races all you really need is to be in a public place, whether on your own or with friends. Pick a random pedestrian, cyclist or even dog nearby and secretly declare a race. To the next lamp post, side street or even all the way home: the finish line is up to you. You can award head starts and time penalties whenever/if they are deserved and do a stealthy celebratory jig when you win.

PERFECT FOR: improving boring walks, feeling superior to strangers.

BALANCING ACTS

ADVENTURERS	LOCATION	DIFFICULTY
👤	🏠	👍👍

Make a game of the mundane by adding a little challenge to the most boring daily tasks. Pretend you're in a finishing class by keeping a book balanced on your head while doing the vacuuming. Tidy up while on one foot. If you're feeling really brave, hold an egg in the crook of your elbow while cleaning the car. Sure, you'll be making a dreary job take longer, but if it's good enough for Mary Poppins, it's good enough for you.

PERFECT FOR: brightening up the housework.

CHANGED DAYS

ADVENTURERS	LOCATION	DIFFICULTY

As the name suggests, this is a game with a difference, as you shun your usual habits and turn your everyday routine on its head. To play Changed Days, you just have to do everything completely differently from how you normally would. Take the car to work? Today you're on the bus. Always have coffee in the morning? Give herbal tea a go instead. Spend your evenings with a good book? Wrap up and go for a walk this time.

PERFECT FOR: amusing yourself, finding new things in your daily life.

The game takes a bit of commitment as your habits are established for a reason, but if you stick with it (as far as you can), you'll discover something interesting about your commute, your job, your local area or yourself that might even change your routine for good.

IT'S A PUZZLE

ADVENTURERS	LOCATION	DIFFICULTY

Puzzles are a relaxing way to spend time and test yourself, but if you're looking for something a little more creative to try, why not make your own puzzle book instead? Then you can have the joy of stumping your friends and family with your homemade brainteasers. You could include:

PERFECT FOR: quiet days at home.

Crosswords

Start with a blank grid: you can either draw your own or copy/print one from online sources. In pencil, fill in words that connect around each other until you have a full network of answers. Then just come up with the clues that lead to each answer and, when finished, rub out the solution for someone else to have a go. Remember to number the clues and the words across and down in the puzzle.

Anagrams

Mix up the letters in common words and phrases. Either leave them jumbled or, for a bit more of a challenge, try to make other words from the letters. You can give clues for any that might be particularly difficult to solve. Use your own name or the names of those around you to personalise the puzzles too.

Word searches

As with your crossword, begin your word search with a blank square grid. Add words randomly around the space in different directions, with some intersecting points. Once you have placed all of your answers, fill in the remaining spaces with random letters. You can pick a theme or write a list or clues to the words hidden in the puzzle to give some context for the solution – or just let your challengers figure it out for themselves!

Games for Two
THERE'S NO 'I' IN TODAY

ADVENTURERS	LOCATION	DIFFICULTY
👤 👤	🏠 🚶	👍

Pick a letter, any letter. Then challenge your
fellow players to have an entire conversation
without using it. Keep it going until someone
uses the letter then choose another to try.
Too easy? After every minute or so, add
another forbidden letter, until all you have
left is a consonant, a vowel and a very
abridged vocabulary. You can also play this game alone to
amuse yourself when bored with a situation. Don't tell anyone
you're limiting your alphabet and see if anyone notices. If they
do, bring them into the game (or deny it all!).

PERFECT FOR:
testing your
conversational
creativity, long
journeys.

NOVEMBER ALFA TANGO OSCAR

ADVENTURERS	LOCATION	DIFFICULTY
👤 👤	🏠 🚶	👍

How long can you keep up a conversation while spelling each word out individually? O.N.E. M.I.N.U.T.E.? T.W.O.? Winner lasts the longest.

PERFECT FOR: car journeys, feeling like a naval officer.

Now, how about while using the NATO alphabet? That's right, have a chat while spelling everything out by the phonetic system used for military communications and giving your surname to call centre operators. It isn't as easy as you might think, especially for the person trying to figure out what's being said. Whoever freezes or takes too long to reply is out of the game.

Go on, give it a Tango Romeo Yankee.

The NATO Alphabet: Alfa, Bravo, Charlie, Delta, Echo, Foxtrot, Golf, Hotel, India, Juliett, Kilo, Lima, Mike, November, Oscar, Papa, Quebec, Romeo, Sierra, Tango, Uniform, Victor, Whiskey, Xray, Yankee, Zulu.

FINGER TWISTER

ADVENTURERS	LOCATION	DIFFICULTY
🧍 🧍	🏠 🚶	👍

Twister – the game of physical contortion and lack of personal space – is a party classic, and if you haven't already played, you're missing a whole lot of awkward giggling. But here's an alternative, in case standard Twister isn't an accessible option or you don't fancy getting quite so cosy with your fellow players.

PERFECT FOR: low-key entertainment, stretching those phalanges.

For Finger Twister, you can buy napkins with the board pre-printed, but it's easy enough to draw out your own bright circles on a sheet of paper with a few crayons and ten minutes to spare. Then you just play the game with your hands instead of your entire body.

To pick which finger to put on which circle, you can:

- make a traditional spinner using card and a paper clip.

- write out scraps of paper with the different colours of
  the circles and scraps identifying the fingers (left
  thumb, right thumb, left finger, right finger). Choose one
  from each bundle per turn.

- let players decide the most difficult combination for
  their opponents.

Each player takes a turn to put and keep their finger on the
given colour, and the game continues with fingers continuously
added around the table, until the whole heap of hands collapses
or someone gets repetitive strain injury.

BOUNCE THE EGG

ADVENTURERS	LOCATION	DIFFICULTY
😊 😊	🏠	👍

Yes, you read that right: for this game the players will be taking it in turns to bounce an egg. Each player must bounce the egg at least once on a table or worktop for their turn to count. You may want to cover the surface in paper first though. There's no real winner of Bounce the Egg, only a loser who misjudges their aim and ends up with yolk on their shoes.

PERFECT FOR:
guaranteed laughs, making a real mess.

How to make a bouncy egg:
Fill a jar or glass with white vinegar and pop in a raw egg (shell and all), ensuring that the egg is completely covered with the liquid. Leave the egg in the vinegar for two to three days, checking in on your science project every so often until the egg starts to become translucent. Carefully empty the egg out of the vinegar and rinse it, wiping off any remaining shell or coating. You now have a bouncy egg!

SPAGHETTI SCRABBLE

ADVENTURERS	LOCATION	DIFFICULTY
👤 👤	🏠	👍 👍

Don't play with your food, they said. But that's why they were always bored. The dinner table can be a great place to find amusement and Spaghetti Scrabble is an easy way to liven up your lunchtime.

PERFECT FOR: turning teatime into playtime, an excuse to eat more carbs.

All you need is a tin of alphabet pasta, two or more diners and enough plates to go around. Share the contents of the can more or less evenly among the players and set a timer (you can pick the duration of the game based on age and spelling ability around the table). When the time is up, each player presents their best word using their given letters, and points are awarded for the longest or most complex effort. The game can continue until someone uses up all of their letters and is declared the winner – or until the dog steals the lot.

PLAYGROUND FUN

ADVENTURERS	LOCATION	DIFFICULTY
👤 👤	🏠 🚶	👍 👍

When did we stop enjoying those games that used to entertain us for hours in the school playground? I'm not sure we ever really did – we just convinced ourselves that we were far too grown-up for such fanciful activities. Well, after trying a fanci-less life for several decades, I'm here to tell you that fanciful is definitely a better option. In case you can't remember the rules to your own favourites, here are a few suggestions that you can play indoors or outdoors. To add to your repertoire further, ask parents and grandparents what they used to play as children; it's a great conversation starter and usually brings back some very joyful memories.

PERFECT FOR: revisiting your youth, connecting with others.

Sardines

If you know Hide and Seek you're halfway to Sardines. One player is the hider, and the rest seekers. But once found, instead of signalling the end of the game, the hider shuffles over and makes room for the person who discovered them. The game continues until all players are squashed into the hiding place together. Cosy.

Hopscotch

Most people would recognise a hopscotch court sketched out in chalk on a pavement, but you can move this popular kids' game indoors, if you want to play but aren't quite ready for a public display of amusement yet. Draw the numbers out on sheets of paper and position them in a conventional Hopscotch layout – a ladder design from one to ten – or in your own format. Throw a coin or pebble onto the first sheet to start the game then hop onto each of the other numbers to the top of the board and back again, stopping (still on one foot) to pick up your marker again before passing it to the next player. On your next turn, you aim for the second square, then the third, and so on, until you're hitting that tenth square and hopping your way back to victory.

The Floor is Lava

A classic children's game that works perfectly at home, The Floor is Lava requires nothing more than robust furniture and a bit of energy, as you try to navigate across the room without your feet (or any other part of you) touching the floor. Well, you don't want lava burns, do you? Just remember not to stand still for too long while planning your next move – as that chair you're on is sinking more every second that you hesitate. Jump! First to touch the carpet is a big losing pile of ash.

⚠PLEASE ADVENTURE RESPONSIBLY!

OUTSIDE IN

ADVENTURERS	LOCATION	DIFFICULTY
👤 👤	🏠	👍 👍

The outdoors doesn't have the monopoly on
fun and games – it just has a better PR
team. Indoors can be just as interesting;
even your own familiar front room can be
made into a sporting arena with just a little
imagination. Try bringing some of these
traditional outside games inside on days
when the weather or your energy levels don't allow
you to put on shoes.

PERFECT FOR:
bad weather
days and
lockdowns.

Frying Pan Tennis

Frying pans make great alternatives when you don't have a
racquet to hand. With a table or chair as a makeshift net and a
sponge or balloon for a ball, you can have a bit of exercise and
practise your volley – and you'll never be rained off court.

Athletics

Half of the fun of this one is in finding creative ways to emulate track and field events without leaving the house. Shot put some rolled up socks, triple jump onto the couch cushions or even set up some small furniture hurdles, if you're feeling brave.

Crazy Golf

Grab a few mugs, some towels, and any cereal boxes or toilet rolls you have lying around and you can build a decent crazy golf course around your house. Add hardy ornaments or tins for slaloms and pick up an umbrella (or an actual club, if you have one) and try to knock the ball into the cups. If you don't have a ball, some scrunched-up tinfoil or paper will work too.

CUTLERY CHAOS

ADVENTURERS	LOCATION	DIFFICULTY
👤 👤	🏠	👍 👍 👍

Cutlery is a great game accessory (and eating aid too, of course), as it doesn't take much imagination to make a meal more fun. To play Cutlery Chaos, prepare lunch as normal or put out a selection of different foods for your guests. Diners can eat anything on the menu that they want but are not allowed to use the correct cutlery for the job. Soup with a fork, spoons for your steak: you can make the game as difficult as you like by picking the most unwieldy foodstuffs and cutlery. Have you ever tried getting a bowl of runny custard into your mouth using only a butter knife? For those silverware experts in the room, add a blindfold to the party or use random household objects as the only cutlery options instead.

PERFECT FOR: upping your cutlery skills but not your table manners.

⚠PLEASE ADVENTURE RESPONSIBLY!

BLUE MONDAY

ADVENTURERS	LOCATION	DIFFICULTY
👤 👤	🏠 🚶	👍 👍 👍

Don't worry – far from reminding you of the saddest day of the year, Blue Monday is a game to cheer up any day. Players pick colours out of a hat (or from an app, if you're modern) and can only wear, drink and eat items of that colour from when the game begins. The person who lasts longest wins. So dig out those pink pants and embrace your new candyfloss diet!

PERFECT FOR: silly fun, making you and all your friends look a bit ridiculous.

DECISIONS, DECISIONS

ADVENTURERS	LOCATION	DIFFICULTY
👤 👤	🏠 🚶	👍 👍 👍

Give yourself a day off from self-direction with a round of Decisions, Decisions. Not the kind of game you want to play with complete strangers, this game is an exercise in trust, as you give up control of every choice you have to make to the other player, for an hour or an entire day, if you're brave enough. How long can you last without choosing your next snack or which nursery to send your first born to? You can play this just for laughs, or add a scoring system if you're the more competitive type – a point awarded for every decision you allow the other player to make for you, and one deducted if you refuse to take on their suggestion. The winner is the person with the highest score, who has relinquished the most control for the duration of the game. But who picks the trophy?

PERFECT FOR: team-building, days when you just don't want to be an adult anymore.

Mix it up:

This is a great game to play long-distance by phone or email with friends and family. Pick a date and a category (for example, food or hobbies) and each make someone else's relevant choices for the day.

Group Games
PICK A SINNER

ADVENTURERS	LOCATION	DIFFICULTY
👤👤👤👤	🏠🚶	👍

Pick a Sinner is best played in a group, either as an icebreaker or when you just want to know a bit more about your mates. All you need is paper and pens, and a mental list of your past misdemeanours. To play, each person writes down a 'sin' they have committed – the sillier the better – and adds it to the pile. Once everyone has added their confession, the papers are spread out for all to read. The players then take it in turns to pick a sin and match it to the sinner. Just remember not to own up to anything you don't want to be public knowledge.

PERFECT FOR: getting to know each other better.

Mix it up:
It's not too difficult to come up with other categories that would work for this game. Here are a few options:

- First/worst jobs.

- Most embarrassing moment.

- Good deeds.

- Happiest memory.

DRAWING GAMES

ADVENTURERS	LOCATION	DIFFICULTY
🧍🧍🧍🧍	🏠	👍

You don't have to be Picasso to enjoy the art of drawing, especially when you make a game of it. There are plenty of drawing activities to try (and it's easy to make up your own too), but here are a few ideas to make a sport of sketching:

PERFECT FOR: family fun.

- Draw someone you know or a celebrity in one minute. Other players try to guess who you have drawn.

- Think of an object for ten seconds and then close your eyes and try to sketch it. Award points to anyone who recognises the object.

- Do a self-portrait using your non-dominant hand. Best portrait wins.

- In pairs, describe a person or object to your partner to draw, without telling them who or what it is. They then try to identify who or what they have drawn.

NOTED

ADVENTURERS	LOCATION	DIFFICULTY
👤👤👤👤	🏠	👍 👍

One to be played with members of your household, Noted isn't a quick party game as such, but more of a sustained campaign of terror against your family. Using sticky notes or scraps of paper, players write out three of the worst chores they can think of then, one at a time or under cover of darkness, find separate hiding spots around the house for each. Whoever finds a note – whether they find it hours, months or years later – has to do the task written on it. The strategy here is to conceal the notes in places that you're least likely to accidentally find them yourself in a few weeks' time, and to come up with ways of surreptitiously directing others towards uncovering them instead. The beauty of this game is that it never has to end. Keep planting notes for evermore and, as long as everyone agrees to do the forfeits they find, you can torment each other until the end of days.

PERFECT FOR: causing family arguments, long-term entertainment.

DEAD OR ALIVE

ADVENTURERS	LOCATION	DIFFICULTY

One that can be tried on your own or turned into a game to play in a group is making your own photo-fits. For those not embroiled in the criminal justice system, photo-fits are the facial reconstruction pictures made to identify potential criminals. But you don't have to be on a Wanted poster to have your own photo-fit.

PERFECT FOR: fun on your own or in a group, feeling like an outlaw.

Using magazines, newspapers, or those annoying leaflets that come through the letterbox every day, cut out strips of the various facial features and make piles of eyes, noses, lips and hairstyles. Like a tame Dr Frankenstein, you can then choose the bits to stick together to look as much like yourself as possible. To make a game, there are options to recreate each other's faces or those of celebrities or people you know. Guess who the players around the table have tried to capture or challenge one another to make certain faces, then pick a winner and laugh at the strange creatures you've all brought to life.

OH MUMMY

ADVENTURERS	LOCATION	DIFFICULTY
𓀀 𓀀 𓀀 𓀀	🏠	👍 👍

Not every home has a chess set or snooker table on hand so here's an entertaining game that uses one of the most basic household objects instead. To play Oh Mummy, separate the group into pairs. One player in each pair, armed with a toilet roll, wraps their partner from head to toe or vice versa as quickly as they can. The winners are the first couple to successfully cover one of their team entirely. But remember to balance speed with caution because one little rip will bring the whole costume apart and you'll have to start all over again.

PERFECT FOR:
fun on a whim.

Mix it up:
If you don't want to use up all of your toilet roll, a more sustainable version of this game can be played with clean bed sheets. In order not to suffocate your fellow players though, rather than mummifying each other, make your best (and quickest) bed sheet toga to win the race.

VICTORIAN GAMES NIGHT

ADVENTURERS	LOCATION	DIFFICULTY

Those Victorians knew how to have a good time. In the days before telly, when streaming services amounted to a guy throwing you in a stream, people spent their evenings amusing themselves with a variety of parlour games. While some games have stuck around for the modern party circuit, others haven't, probably for good reason.

PERFECT FOR: livening up the usual games night.

Snapdragon

A health and safety nightmare of a game, Snapdragon is set up by laying out raisins and nuts on a plate or tray (that won't melt or catch fire), drowning them in brandy and setting the whole soup alight. Players take turns to pinch a dried piece of fruit from the inferno and eat their flaming spoils. The winner, I imagine, is the person sitting closest to the fire extinguisher.

Are You There, Moriarty?

If you like your games violent, the Victorians have you covered. In Are You There, Moriarty?, two players are blindfolded and lie face down, brandishing rolled up newspapers, slippers or other not-too-dangerous weapons. Head to head but around an arm's length apart, the players start the game with the question, 'Are you there, Moriarty?' At the answer, 'Yes', the first player attempts to hit the second with their weapon of choice. The players switch between being the smacker and the smacked until someone leaves in a huff.

Forfeits

All you need for a good round of Forfeits is a couple of people with material possessions they don't want to lose. Everyone in the game hands over a prized object to the player with the role of Auctioneer, who then decides on a price for each item to be returned to its owner. If you don't want to be forced to do 20 press-ups or run naked across the back garden then you probably shouldn't have brought your favourite pet to the party.

GAME OF GAMES

ADVENTURERS	LOCATION	DIFFICULTY
🧍🧍🧍🧍	🏠	👍 👍 👍

Hopefully by now you'll agree that games are wonderful and can quickly turn a dull day around. For those times though when you fancy something completely different, you can play Game of Games to try creating your own instead.

PERFECT FOR:
when you've played all the other games in this book.

Original and imaginative games can be tricky to design but it's easy – and much more fun – to make up truly terrible games. So why not make a game of making up dreadful games? Everyone has to come up with a rubbish idea, then you pick the best bad game and the winner gets a head start when you all inevitably play their terrible invention straight afterwards.

Tip: start with an awful pun and the game will normally follow!

For example:

Tickled Onions

One player – preferably the most ticklish person among you – puts on all the clothes they can find. The rest of the group take it in turns to try to tickle the player to make them laugh. After every turn, the player takes off one layer. If they manage not to laugh by the time they're down to their normal clothes again, they win!

Musical Pears

Place a bowl of fruit in the middle of a room, with one fewer piece than there are players. The group circles the bowl and, when the music stops, everyone tries to grab a piece of fruit from the selection as quickly as possible. The player without a snack is out.

PICTURE IT

ADVENTURERS	LOCATION	DIFFICULTY
👤👤👤👤	🏠	👍👍👍

Dig all of those old photographs out of the cupboard and prepare to get creative. There's no easier way to entertain friends than by embarrassing yourself – and pictures of you in a paddling pool or shoulder pads will usually do the work for you. Ask players to bring along a selection of photos too, if you think they'll join in, and then at least you'll manage to squeeze in a few giggles too.

PERFECT FOR: family gatherings, team-building.

The game: everyone chooses a photo from the pile – or you can pick them for each other to make it more difficult – and one by one the players have to recreate their image using only what they can find around them and their own bodies. Help can be enlisted if the scene features more than one character. The most realistic or comical version of a given photo wins.

You can also play this game using images from magazines, film posters or album covers if you don't want to share your past fashion mistakes with your guests.

CHALLENGES

What's life without a little challenge? Easy and comfortable, you might say. And you'd be right. But adding a little bit of discomfort to your day can do wonders for your outlook, your wellbeing and your anecdotes. You don't have to climb a mountain or become a surgeon to test yourself either. There are plenty of ways to stretch your mental and physical abilities within easy reach of your own front door. But you can move them slightly further away, if you fancy the extra mileage. Sometimes just looking at your own world from a different angle will help you to see it anew so prepare to stand on your head and squint wildly in the direction of your next adventure.

A FEW OF MY FAVOURITE THINGS

ADVENTURERS	LOCATION	DIFFICULTY
🧑	🏠	👍

You love ketchup, you love ice cream: have a spoonful of ketchup ice cream. Mixing together your favourite foods, hobbies, even books, can provide some interesting – if not particularly tasty – entertainment. Alternate between the pages of two of your best-loved novels. Combine great starters and desserts on the same plate. Watch a good film while listening to another. They won't all be natural bedfellows, but you might just invent a new classic. Here are some combinations to get you started:

PERFECT FOR: pointless entertainment.

- Pickled onion tea.

- Pride and Dracula.

- Toast and jelly beans.

- Mustard gin.

- Pottery bowling.

- Close Encounters of Rambo.

STROLL ON THE WILD SIDE

ADVENTURERS	LOCATION	DIFFICULTY
👤	🏠	👍

Don your best fedora and head to the park or even just your garden to take a local safari. There's more wildlife in your area than you imagine, and even if there aren't lions or tigers or bears nearby, there are still creatures that will have you saying 'oh my' right on your doorstep. Check out nature guides for your area to find out which particular birds or bees you might have to learn about, make a list and see how many you can tick off in one afternoon. Take binoculars if you have them, but your phone camera, a wildlife checklist and a healthy dose of childish wonderment are enough to turn your local patch into an Attenborough special.

PERFECT FOR:
lazy days
and Sundays.

DEAR ME

ADVENTURERS	LOCATION	DIFFICULTY
🧑	🏠 🚶	👍

What would you say to your younger self, if you could go back in time? Stop worrying about things that won't matter in a week's time? Please don't get that awful tattoo? Step away from the peroxide? Whatever your advice would be, writing it out in a letter to your past self can be a really interesting exercise in addressing unresolved issues or just laughing at your own decisions and habits.

PERFECT FOR: an afternoon of reflection.

Now, what about future you? Thinking about what you've learned in the last ten years – and the advice you have just given teenage you – jot a note to the you of a decade ahead. Afterwards, either tuck your letter away in an envelope to be opened on a specific date down the line or keep it by your bed, read it every morning and challenge yourself to live by your own counsel.

BIRTHDAY SUIT

ADVENTURERS	LOCATION	DIFFICULTY
👤	🏠	👍 👍

Rummage through the back of your wardrobe for this throwback challenge, as you dress like the year you were born. Not how you would have dressed back then, you understand; nobody needs to see you in a baby-grow and bib. Channel your parents' heyday style, dig out old photos and recreate the looks. Alter your modern garments with belts or safety pins to pay homage to the styles of the past, and remind yourself how lucky you are not to remember those early years of your life.

PERFECT FOR: an easy, at-home activity with a few laughs along the way.

Turn the fun into a game by involving the whole family: quickest to don the fashions of their year of birth wins. (But we're all losers with this one really.)

PLACE OF SPADES

ADVENTURERS	LOCATION	DIFFICULTY
𐐒	⌂	👍 👍

Next time you have a spare hour and a
bucket-load of patience, find a pack of
playing cards and try building yourself a
house. Thankfully, it doesn't need to be
structurally sound; you won't be applying for
insurance or anything.

PERFECT FOR:
a sit-down
adventure.

Use a flat surface – nobody needs an extra hurdle on this one –
and start with two cards. Prop them together so they are touching
at the top in a triangle. Make another two of these triangles,
evenly spaced next to your first, to create your base. Take a deep
breath, steady your hands, and balance a card flat on top of the
points of your first two triangles. Repeat this across the row to
make a floor for your next layer. Now build more triangles on top.
Keep going until you reach the top of your pyramid or it all
collapses around you.

Start a swear jar; you'll fill it by the time you've finished.

CRAZY COLOURING

ADVENTURERS	LOCATION	DIFFICULTY
👤	🏠 🚶	👍 👍

If you like nothing more than everything being in its rightful place, here's a real challenge for you. Pick up a nice colouring book and some crayons or pencils and try colouring outside the lines. You can follow the design and colour around it or just ignore the lines altogether and scribble all the way through them. If colouring is mindful, this is mindless, and makes you feel like a rebel on a very small scale.

PERFECT FOR: a very small act of rebellion.

ARMCHAIR ALPHABET

ADVENTURERS	LOCATION	DIFFICULTY
🧍	🏠	👍 👍

Look around your home and what do you see? The same old boring ornaments and clutter. No! You see your very own alphabet in potentia. Test your imagination as you look at your surroundings differently and make letters from household objects. Those scissors make a great X. The banana rotting in the fruit bowl is just a C in disguise. Before long you'll be seeing letters everywhere you look.

PERFECT FOR:
seeing your trash as treasure.

Try spelling out your name or a favourite quote or create the entire alphabet from one room for an extra element of challenge. You always said that novelty shoe horn would come in handy for something.

JE NE REGRETTE RIEN

ADVENTURERS	LOCATION	DIFFICULTY

PERFECT FOR: broadening your mind, being smug in multiple dialects.

There's no denying that learning a new language is a challenge, but it's one worth all the effort. From improving communication skills to boosting creativity, being multilingual is a real asset in anyone's arsenal. Whether or not you're a world traveller, there's still good reason to explore languages, and you don't have to join a class to get started, although you'll benefit hugely from native instruction if you do. Books, apps, and online resources are all options for complete beginners, but if you're not ready to start learning sign language or German just yet, you can challenge yourself to learn a sentence, or just 'hello', in ten different languages or give something like Klingon or Elvish a go first. They may not be useful in everyday life, but they'll boost your brain anyway.

YOU: THE MUSICAL

ADVENTURERS	LOCATION	DIFFICULTY
👤	🏠 🚶	👍 👍

Live like Dorothy for a day in the starring role of the musical of your own life. Which songs would be on the soundtrack of You? Pick tracks that have meant a lot to you over the years or that bookmark important events in your history. Ask older family members if they have any memories of your favourite childhood tunes. Find out what was at the top of the charts on your every birthday (there are lots of websites to help you out with just a quick date search) and add them to the list. Make up a playlist – or a mix tape, if you're old school – and spend the day boring everyone with the tracks of your years.

PERFECT FOR:
celebrating your life, forcing everyone else to do the same.

AROUND THE WORLD IN EIGHTY PLATES

ADVENTURERS	LOCATION	DIFFICULTY
☖	⌂	👍 👍

When you are tired of steak pie Sundays and Friday night fish and chips, change up your menu with an around the world buffet night. Source the most interesting ingredients from different places and cultures, test your cookery skills with new recipes (or just buy the tinned version for quickness) and eat your way around the world. Invite your family and friends to guess where each dish is from or go all out and make little flags for your dishes from the appropriate countries.

PERFECT FOR: introducing new food to your diet, livening up meal times.

You can stretch this out over a week or even the year by choosing a different area's tastes to explore at a time. Add in traditional local beverages too, if you really want to embrace the holiday spirit.

REMEMBER, REMEMBER

ADVENTURERS	LOCATION	DIFFICULTY
👤	🏠🚶	👍 👍

Forget your rock-hard abs for five minutes and give your brain a proper workout instead. It's easy to forget that your memory needs regular maintenance too so throw on a sweatband, flex your mental muscles and try to memorise a list or sequence throughout the day. Here are a few options you could start with:

PERFECT FOR: stretching your mind.

- 100 digits of pi.

- The order of a pack of cards.

- Your favourite poem – or someone else's to impress them.

- The periodic table.

- World capitals and flags.

- Ingredients of your shampoo.

- Birthdays of your loved ones (probably the most useful option).

HOME IS WHERE THE ART IS

ADVENTURERS	LOCATION	DIFFICULTY
👤	🏠	👍 👍

We've all been to museums and thought, 'I could do better than that', right? Well, now is the time to prove it. Plan and develop your very own art exhibition from items around your home and impress your patrons with your remarkable taste.

PERFECT FOR: jazzing up your walls, saving you a trip to the local gallery.

Gather together some items of more or less artistic merit from your attic, junk drawer or fridge door. Include handmade works, unusual knick-knacks or just favourite family mementoes. Display the artworks in one space or distribute them across rooms for a more interactive experience. Write up museum labels to attach to each object. Ask the artists to name their work and give you an insight into their process or just make it all up in your best art historian jargon. Commission the youngsters in the family to create bespoke pieces, grab Granny's latest cross-stitch, even commandeer the dog's slobbery toys for a standalone work. You never know, Rover's 'Chewed Slipper in Saliva' might just be the next big thing in modern art.

CITIZEN BRAIN

ADVENTURERS	LOCATION	DIFFICULTY
😕	🏠 🏃	👍 👍

Do you know who built that famous cathedral in the capital? Or how long ago a local battle was fought? Could you spot your national animal across a crowded room? Prove you are a true **[INSERT YOUR NATIONALITY HERE]** by taking your home country's citizenship exam. You can test your knowledge of your country of origin (or any other) online by searching for practice questions, and spend an hour reminding yourself how much or little you have to learn about your birthplace.

PERFECT FOR: learning more about your culture and customs.

BURNING DOWN THE HOUSE

ADVENTURERS	LOCATION	DIFFICULTY
👤	🏠	👍 👍

Unless you live near a big, bad wolf, building a house out of matchsticks is a perfectly acceptable practice. Be warned, this can be fiddly and you will literally be playing with matches so it's best to do this if you're of the right disposition.

PERFECT FOR: using up all your spare matches and patience.

Lay down a square of around eight matchsticks evenly spaced on a level and heatproof surface, such as a baking tray. On top, place another eight matchsticks, running across your bottom layer from side to side. Continue to alternate these two layers until you have built a cube. You can fill in the gaps with more matchsticks to stabilise the house and add triangles of balanced matches to form a roof on top. Or you can leave it just as a box and move on to the fun part.

Admire your handiwork for a moment, then carefully move it to a safe place outdoors, light it at the bottom, and watch your entire afternoon burn to nothing.

WASTE NOT WANT NOT

ADVENTURERS	LOCATION	DIFFICULTY
😊	🏠 🚶	👍 👍

Wage your own small war on waste by challenging yourself to go plastic-free for a week (or longer). We all know the problems that our disposable culture causes, and taking small steps to reduce your contribution to landfill is a worthwhile pursuit and a good test of your creative thinking.
Here are a few tips, in case you don't know where to start:

PERFECT FOR: making small changes, doing your bit for the world.

- Take reusable water bottles, coffee cups and cutlery with you instead of accepting the plastic versions from takeaway cafes.

- Make your own toothpaste and avoid buying the plastic tubes (see page 80 for recipe).

- Choose loose fruit and vegetables in the supermarket. Keep them together in mesh or canvas bags rather than the throwaway alternatives.

- Buy or make wax wraps to store and cover food instead of using cling film.

- Use bars of soap rather than bottles of hand-wash. Shampoos are also available in bars to replace your regular haircare bottles too.

- Question your choices in the supermarket and, wherever possible, go for the plastic-free option.

SET THE RECORD STRAIGHT

ADVENTURERS	LOCATION	DIFFICULTY
🧍	🏠 🚶	👍 👍 👍

You know you're extraordinary, I know you're extraordinary. But have you ever tried showing the world just how extraordinary you are? You could break a record in your sleep – noisiest snore, longest nap in an awkward position – so challenge yourself to setting a few in your waking hours too.

PERFECT FOR: achieving something silly, finding new talents and showing them off.

Browse the different records online or just make up your own then spend a few fun hours figuring out where your talents really lie. Or go the official route and apply to Guinness for your record of choice. Then all you need to do is practise! Here are some of my favourite records to start with:

- Most underpants worn at once.

- Farthest distance walked on toe knuckles.

- Most dried peas moved using a straw in 30 seconds.

- Biggest conga line of dogs.

OPEN DOORS

ADVENTURERS	LOCATION	DIFFICULTY

Fancy yourself as a bit of a covert operative? Then test out your skills with a spot of lock-picking. Put down the balaclava please, we are not dabbling in housebreaking, but learning to pick locks is great for challenging your hand–eye coordination and manual dexterity. Full locksmith kits are available to buy, as are beginners' sets for interested hobbyists, which come with tension wrenches and clear padlocks so you can see the mechanism as you work. Or you can go full Miss Marple and use a hairpin on your own front door instead – it might take longer but the satisfaction if it works is timeless. Plus you'll soon find out the weaknesses in your own home security system as a costly bonus. There are loads of online tutorials and written resources if you want to learn this skill properly, but just jiggling a hat pin in a handcuff is a fun introduction to your new hobby.

PERFECT FOR: improving manual dexterity, never being locked out again.

ORDER, ORDER

ADVENTURERS	LOCATION	DIFFICULTY
👤	🏠	👍 👍 👍

Let's face it, life is chaotic. Bringing a little organisation to your home, then, can be therapeutic. Sorry, did I say 'a little', I meant a metric truckload of organisation. What I'm talking about here is the go hard or go home of organising: alphabetising your house. Yes, your entire house.

PERFECT FOR: pretending you have control over something.

Start small with a bookcase – maybe even make a card catalogue, if you're going for the full library experience – then move to your wardrobe and kitchen cupboards. Put things in A–Z order or pick a classification system that works better for you, but stick to it throughout every part of the house.

Soon you'll be buying a label maker and rearranging the family tree in height order. Afterwards, admire your handiwork, embrace being able to find everything for a few hours, then mess it all up and go back to your normal, anarchic life.

(Please organise responsibly. This is just a silly activity to spend a day doing. Don't try to organise your whole world; it will drive you crazy.)

WORM FOOD

ADVENTURERS	LOCATION	DIFFICULTY
👤	🏠 🚶	👍 👍 👍

PERFECT FOR: testing your palate, proving you'd survive the apocalypse.

Sometimes traditional snacks just aren't what you want. They're too, I don't know, tasty or whatever. These are the days when you could challenge yourself to give a different delicacy a go and put bugs in your lunchbox instead. Edible insects are being hailed as humanity's salvation and lots of the world's population already have them on the daily menu so don't be any later to the party and add a locust or two to your sandwich today. Dried or juicy, turned into flour or pasta, seasoned and coated or just as they come: mealworms, locusts, crickets and the like are available in some supermarkets and online for all you budding bug eaters to scoff.

If insects are already part of your diet, why not challenge yourself to try other unfamiliar delicacies instead? Research food stuffs from around the world and introduce your taste buds to something new and adventurous today.

GYM BUNNIES

ADVENTURERS	LOCATION	DIFFICULTY
👤	🏠	👍 👍 👍

If you feel like getting physical with your challenges, but the gym is too far away and you'd be tired by the time you walked there, give human weights a whirl*. Line your family up in size order and – over a nice cushioned surface – see how many you can lift. If your loved ones aren't willing or it

PERFECT FOR:
home exercise,
a bit of fun
with the family.

would cause offence, this can be done with household objects and pets. Count how many repetitions you can do with each kitchen chair or measure how far off the ground you budged Benji. Be careful, obviously: this is an adventure, not an excuse to go to A & E. So far, my personal best is one small auntie and a particularly greedy Chihuahua.

*Don't actually whirl them though, you don't want your barbell vomiting.

⚠PLEASE ADVENTURE RESPONSIBLY!

PUT YOUR FUNNY
WHERE YOUR MOUTH IS

ADVENTURERS	LOCATION	DIFFICULTY
🧍	🏠 🚶	👍 👍 👍

PERFECT FOR: building confidence, shattering confidence.

Everyone says you're hilarious, but do they mean it? There's one way to check if they're laughing with you or at you: sign up for an open mic night. Terrifying, exhilarating and, at times, painful to watch, open mic events are run in cafes and clubs to allow budding performers to test their material on willing audiences. Find one in your area (or outside it, if you don't fancy seeing anyone you know) and put your name down for a slot on the schedule. Turn up prepared with your material, gather your courage, and have fun trying to make people laugh.

If you can't get along to an event, organise your own. Either online or with a few chairs and a brush for a microphone, you could soon be entertaining your social circle of an evening. Invite your friends to join in too, and soon you'll have a full programme of comedy, music and spoken word performances to endure. Sorry, enjoy.

DOUBLE TROUBLE

ADVENTURERS	LOCATION	DIFFICULTY
👤 👤	🏠 🏃	👍 👍

Clothes twinning is not just for girl bands from the eighties; you can do it too. Although you won't look quite as bodacious while you do, of course. Turn your wardrobe into a test of creativity with one of these silly activities:

PERFECT FOR:
looking daft
and loving it.

- Team up with another member of your family or social circle – preferably one you don't normally share clothes with – and dress in as matching an outfit as you can. Wait to see if anyone notices.

- Challenge your household to all dress like someone else in the family. Pair up and dress the same or take the individual route and guess who each other is imitating. Try not to offend anyone with your choice of outfit – Grandpa doesn't wear those orthopaedic shoes by choice, you know.

- Dress the same as your pet for the day. You don't need the collar, unless you really want it.

BEAT THE HEAT

ADVENTURERS	LOCATION	DIFFICULTY

Chilli eating contests, much like the fiery little fruits themselves, are sprouting up all over, and if you fancy your taste buds' chances against the hot stuff, get yourself along and join in. For those of us who prefer not to share our discomfort with an audience of strangers, it's easy enough to set up an at-home competition for friends.

PERFECT FOR: a group activity for brave diners.

You can use different types of chillies themselves or hot sauces, if they are easier to source; just line them up in order from mildest to hottest (look up the Scoville scale, which ranks spiciness, to help with this) and see who can make it furthest along the table, taking a little bit of each at a time. Have milk on hand, just in case, to alleviate the burning sensation, but anyone who reaches for it is disqualified from the rest of the challenge.

Please don't take this one too far: competitiveness is all well and good until someone ends up having their stomach pumped.

⚠PLEASE ADVENTURE RESPONSIBLY!

DON'T STARE

ADVENTURERS	LOCATION	DIFFICULTY
🧍🧍🧍	🏠 🚶	👍

When you can't decide whose turn it is to take the bins out, and you have plenty of time to settle the matter, challenge your housemate or partner to a reverse staring contest. Sit facing each other, just close enough to be slightly uncomfortable, close your eyes and start the match. First to open their eyes again loses. Without touching them, do or say whatever you can to encourage your opponent to twitch those lids. You'll need an adjudicator too, of course, or a pair of cheats might never end the game!

PERFECT FOR: resolving silly disputes, sending everyone involved to sleep.

ACTIVITIES

When you are tired of doing nothing, doing something is a great alternative. But what to do? Being active doesn't have to mean star jumping across the street; keeping your brain and hands busy is just as important to maintaining wellbeing and a healthy interest in the world. With only a few random items from around your house and a decent dose of imagination, you can keep yourself entertained for hours without spending a penny. Toilet breaks are recommended though.

Here's the deal: I'll bring the ideas, you bring the cardboard and googly eyes. Let's get started.

BOATS IN THE BATH

ADVENTURERS	LOCATION	DIFFICULTY
👤	🏠	👍

Turn your bathtub into a jolly regatta by saving up your wine bottle corks and making them into pretty boats. Don your best captain's hat and prepare to set sail.

PERFECT FOR: entertaining yourself quietly, justifying wine bottles.

How to:

1. Use elastic bands to secure together three or four corks side by side. If the corks are tapered, alternate the direction they are facing to even out the shape.

2. Design a sail from a piece of card or paper, and use a skewer or toothpick as a mast to attach it to your corks.

3. Make as many boats as your drinking habits can provide, fill your bath and watch them float.

CHIN UP

ADVENTURERS	LOCATION	DIFFICULTY
🧑	🏠	👍

If you have never painted your chin then hung upside down over the back of a kitchen chair pretending that your chin is a face, what have you been doing with your Sunday afternoons all your life? To make a chinhead all you need is a chin – your own will do

PERFECT FOR:
silly fun,
making use of
tiny hats.

nicely – and some make-up or face paints. Accessories help to complete the illusion so if you have sunglasses or googly eyes around the house, bring them to the party.

Use a mirror or enlist some help to set up your look: eyes at the bottom of your face, a moustache under your lower lip, maybe even a tiny hat stuck to the underside of your chin. Just copy your own face the wrong way around if that helps. It will all look a bit strange until you dangle your head upside down then voila! Your chinhead is alive and your entire day is spent miming songs and trying to drink convincingly without drowning yourself. Have fun!

Tip: For a less acrobatic reveal, use a camera to take photos and turn them upside down instead.

GREEN FINGERS

ADVENTURERS	LOCATION	DIFFICULTY
🧍	🏠 🚶	👍

Bring a little nature into your home using some crayons or coloured pencils and what the local trees have to offer. Raid your garden or a park for leaves of different shapes and textures and sit in the sunshine – or retreat to the comfort of your couch – and cover them with a blank sheet of paper. Rub your crayon over the paper and watch the delicate patterns of the leaves appear. Overlap the leaves or use a variety of colours to adapt your artwork.

PERFECT FOR:
a restful half hour.

FACE IT

ADVENTURERS	LOCATION	DIFFICULTY
😟	🏠 🚶	👍

If you don't already have a favourite side of your face, you will after trying this activity. We all know our faces aren't symmetrical, so why not find out what they would look like if they were? There are apps and online options to try this digitally but you can do it yourself with two mirrors – one small, one bigger. Hold the smaller mirror in the middle of your face so that the edge of the glass is against your nose, running vertically down through your forehead and chin. You might have to change the angle of the mirror to get the full effect. Now check out your reflection in the bigger mirror and be pleasantly surprised or utterly horrified. Either way, your face is much better as it is, I promise.

PERFECT FOR: appreciating your own beauty, laughing at everyone else's.

Try this with your pet cat or dog to have some harmless fun at the poor creature's expense.

TOWEL OFF

ADVENTURERS	LOCATION	DIFFICULTY
👤	🏠	👍 👍

What is the point of a towel if not to fashion it into the shape of a lobster and display it atop your bedspread? Towel art has been popularised over the years by overworked chambermaids, but you can recreate the hotel feel with your own bath-sheets by learning to fold towel animals at home. For the more complex designs you'll need multiple towels and a good degree in engineering but try this relatively simple swan for starters:

PERFECT FOR: impressing guests, pretending you're on holiday.

How to:

1. Spread a large towel out with the long side facing you. Fold the two corners at the top in to meet at the middle.

2. Roll the two folded edges in towards the middle until they resemble an arrow.

3. Lift up the point and bend the arrow into a Z to form the neck. Manoeuver your swan so that it sits upright.

4. You can add a rolled-up hand towel on top of the wings to create a fuller body shape.

JUMP FOR JOY

ADVENTURERS	LOCATION	DIFFICULTY
👤	🏠 🚶	👍 👍

It's the age-old question: do we click our heels because we are happy or are we happy because we click our heels? Either way, bring joy to any old day by giving it a try. Just jump as high as you can and bring those heels together in mid-air. Click to the side, click sitting down, click on your way to work – and with each click feel a little more like Fred Astaire.

PERFECT FOR: a cheerer-upper, falling on your backside repeatedly.

⚠️PLEASE ADVENTURE RESPONSIBLY!

DIY DENTISTRY

ADVENTURERS	LOCATION	DIFFICULTY
🧑	🏠	👍 👍

Smile: here's a quick and cheap activity that will leave you feeling fresh and ready to dazzle. There are various recipes for homemade toothpaste available, but with just a little bicarbonate of soda and some water, you can make this very simple version in only a minute or two. For a small sample to try out, use around a tablespoon of bicarbonate of soda in a small glass then add cold water until the mixture forms a paste of your chosen consistency. Slop it onto your toothbrush and open wide!

PERFECT FOR: low-cost hygiene.

GIVE A LITTLE BIT

ADVENTURERS	LOCATION	DIFFICULTY
👤	🏠 🚶	👍 👎

Research consistently shows that giving of yourself to others in even the smallest ways can have huge positive impact on your own wellbeing. And you don't have to empty your bank account or energy stores to do it.

PERFECT FOR:
feeling like a hero.

Time

Volunteering might not seem like the most glamorous adventure, but it can make your spare time feel a whole lot more worthwhile than thumb-twiddling ever could. You can help out with anything from administration to tree-planting; the variety of roles on offer is endless so if you really feel like a challenge, throw your name in the hat for a task you've never tried before and learn on the job.

Check out your local community and volunteering service for opportunities in your area.

Blood

Giving blood, if you're able, is a great way to spend an hour and you can pat yourself on the back afterwards for helping save lives. Wait until after you've had the free tea and biscuit though or you might feel a bit lightheaded with the exertion. Donating the red stuff is not as scary as you think, it makes you feel like an absolute hero and it's the best gift we can give another person, without costing ourselves more than a bus fare to do it.

Food

Next time you're in the supermarket, consider adding one more tin or box to your trolley. Local food banks will be grateful for anything appropriate that you can hand in, and you probably won't really notice the added item on your receipt anyway. Usually canned goods, toiletries and long-life products are very much appreciated.

PENCIL SHARPENER

ADVENTURERS	LOCATION	DIFFICULTY
👤	🏠	👍 👍

Did you know you can make art with pencils? I know, amazing, right? But aside from sketching your best still life, you can also use pencils as a medium for carving. Skilled carvers can create incredible and intricate sculptures on the tip of a pencil's lead, using the right tools and years of practice. But for beginners, just find a sharp craft knife, raid your Crayola kit, and start hacking (carefully) into that coloured point. A heart is a great shape to start with, but have a sharpener and some patience on hand because your heart will break as many times as the lead does.

PERFECT FOR: upgrading your craft skills, testing your eyesight.

⚠ PLEASE ADVENTURE RESPONSIBLY!

CATCH THE SUN

ADVENTURERS	LOCATION	DIFFICULTY
☖	⌂	👍 👍

Even if it's grey outside, you can brighten up your windows by making your own stained-glass-effect sun-catchers. Gather together your favourite colours of tissue paper, some white glue and freezer paper (plastic document wallets or non-stick baking paper will do the job too), and try this quick and family-friendly project.

PERFECT FOR:
livening up
a dull view.

How to:

1. Cut or rip your tissue paper into pieces (no smaller than an inch long or it will all become a bit fiddly).

2. Spread a layer of white glue on the freezer paper. You can dilute the glue if it's too thick.

3. Cover the glue with random, overlapping pieces of tissue paper until you're happy with the pattern then leave to dry.

4. Peel off the freezer paper and cut out your preferred shape for your sun-catcher from the dried tissue paper piece.

5. Stick it to your window with a little tape or string and watch the sunlight stream through.

FINGERPRINT FUN

ADVENTURERS	LOCATION	DIFFICULTY
🧍	🏠	👍 👍

Maybe you have already had your fingerprints taken, maybe you haven't. This is a safe space: no judgement here. But have you ever taken your own just for fun? With a pencil, scribble a small square on a blank piece of paper, going over the same area

PERFECT FOR:
bringing out your inner law enforcer.

again and again to build up the residue. Press your finger firmly onto the square to transfer the pencil markings to your skin. Stick clear tape over the same area of your finger then pull it away gently. Place the tape sticky side down onto white paper to reveal your fingerprint. Take a full set for everyone in the house and next time a biscuit goes missing, you'll find the culprit before they've digested the evidence.

RANSOM DEVIL

ADVENTURERS	LOCATION	DIFFICULTY
🧍	🏠	👍 👍

You don't have to be up to no good to appreciate a well-designed ransom note. And as long as you're not using it for evil, you can have some fun writing a message in this unusual format. If you happen to earn some minor reward from it, then who can complain?

PERFECT FOR: a harmless bit of mischief.

Think up what you want to say in your note beforehand then cut all the letters you need from magazines, newspapers and leaflets. Different sizes, colours and fonts make for a more authentic look. Stick them to a sheet of paper in a haphazard manner then leave it for your recipient to find. Please don't send this in the post to anyone though; you don't want to be causing any accidental concern.

Example: I HAVE YOUR PHONE. IF YOU WANT TO SEE IT AGAIN, BRING CAKE.

TOUR YOUR OWN TOWN

ADVENTURERS	LOCATION	DIFFICULTY
🧑	🏠 🚶	👍 👍

When you fancy a bit of sightseeing, but distant lands are out of reach, try being a resident tourist instead. Most of us are guilty of not exploring our local landscape in the same way as we would a daytrip destination, so make a list of all the nearby places of

PERFECT FOR: a cheap day out.

interest and challenge yourself to visit each one. If you've recently moved into a new neighbourhood, borrow a guidebook for the area and you'll soon be out discovering what's right on your doorstep. Take along a friend and become a tour guide for the day as you introduce them to the wonders of your town. Even the local recycling centre or greasy spoon cafe can become a landmark with the right description and a bit of imagination.

ARTY PARTY

ADVENTURERS	LOCATION	DIFFICULTY
👤	🏠	👍 👍

PERFECT FOR: learning new skills or perfecting old ones.

Whether or not you're a budding Picasso, painting can be a mindful and compelling hobby. But even if scribbled stick people are the extent of your artistic talent, you can still create something beautiful, especially if the Old Masters have already done the work for you. Pick up a book of famous paintings or find some online that you like and try your hand at copying them. After all, imitation is the highest form of flattery and you're probably not going to enter the world of art fraud straight afterwards. Are you?

GUERRILLAS IN THE MIST

ADVENTURERS	LOCATION	DIFFICULTY
🧍	🚶	👍 👍

For all you rebels without a cause, put your practical skills to use and make your community a little brighter with some guerrilla action. Before you put on the war paint and camouflage gear though, this is not a call to arms, unless those arms are wearing a

PERFECT FOR: sneaky fun.

woolly cardigan or carrying a trowel. Guerrilla knitting or gardening is the practice of reclaiming abandoned or bleak landscapes, either to make them look more appealing or as a form of protest. Get involved by digging out your rake or yarn and plant seedlings in a pothole or make jumpers for goalposts. But don't get caught, as this is technically an act of graffiti, albeit a temporary one.

LAVA PALAVER

ADVENTURERS	LOCATION	DIFFICULTY
👤	🏠	👍 👍

Throw yourself back to the seventies with
your own homemade lava lamp.

How to:

PERFECT FOR:
feeling like a
science teacher,
retro styling.

1. Quarter fill a jar or glass with water
   then top it up with cooking oil, leaving
   an inch of space at the top.

2. Add food colouring in your favourite colour or some
   glitter if you prefer a little sparkle.

3. Break up an effervescent tablet (an Alka-Seltzer or
   fizzy Vitamin C tablet will work) and add some or all of
   the chunks to the mix.

4. You can place a small candle behind the glass to
   illuminate the effect then watch and wait as your lava
   comes bubbling to life.

TEA LIGHTS

ADVENTURERS	LOCATION	DIFFICULTY
👤	🏠	👍 👍

Dig out that old dinner set your great aunt gave you four anniversaries ago, dust off a cup and saucer and prepare to make something to give her straight back.

PERFECT FOR: turning tat into treasure.

How to:

1. You'll need some wax flakes or pellets, wicks and an old pot that you don't mind ruining.

2. Hold the other end of the wick straight up or wrap it around a straw or skewer balanced across your cup's lip so it doesn't fall into the wax.

3. Melt the wax on a low heat then pour it into the cup, making sure the wick stays in the centre and does not fall in.

4. Leave the candle to set overnight on a level surface.

⚠PLEASE ADVENTURE RESPONSIBLY!

A YEAR OF YOU

ADVENTURERS	LOCATION	DIFFICULTY
👤	🏠	👍 👍

If you're superstitious about throwing away old photos, you can always turn them into something useful and palm them off to other people. I mean, give them as beautiful presents. Stick the pictures to a glittery piece of card and add a hoop of string at the top for hanging. Now just attach a mini calendar: wait until after January has been and gone and you'll pick one up for pennies in an office supplies shop. Hand them in to favourite family members and watch them display your handiwork proudly on the kitchen wall. Or chuck them in the bin, but at least the bad luck will be theirs if they do.

PERFECT FOR: making a thoughtful gift, clearing out photo albums.

WHAT A BALLOON!

ADVENTURERS	LOCATION	DIFFICULTY
🧍	🏠	👍 👍 👍

You don't have to sport a red nose and oversized shoes to make a balloon sculpture. You can, but you don't have to. Balloon modelling is endlessly entertaining, utterly pointless, and you'll give yourself a series of little frights as you twist that misshapen

PERFECT FOR:
solo or group fun,
a new party piece.

poodle into glorious existence. Is it going to burst on this twist or the next? Who knows? But you'll have a lot of fun finding out.

Tips:

- Use balloons specifically for modelling, if you can, as these are sturdier and won't burst as easily. Invest in a cheap pump or you'll run out of breath before you've made your first masterpiece.

- Don't fully inflate the balloon – leave about an inch uninflated to give you enough room to manipulate it into shape.

- To make a basic twist, hold the balloon in one hand and pinch and turn a section a little further down with the other. Continue to hold both ends or the twist will loosen.

- To secure a twist, make three basic twists as though forming sausages with the balloon. Now hold two of the sausages side by side and turn their twists together to lock them into each other. It's fiddly, but it works.

- Use your new skills to create the most impressive balloon animal you can imagine.

THE JIG IS UP

ADVENTURERS	LOCATION	DIFFICULTY
👤	🏠	👍 👍 👍

Cutting up a favourite photo might seem like an offence, but not if you make something fun from the parts. There are plenty of businesses that will turn your snaps into beautiful jigsaws professionally, but in the spirit of adventure, try making your own instead.

PERFECT FOR:
a bespoke gift, making a mess of a treasured snapshot.

How to:

1. Using a photo that you don't mind ruining (just in case!), draw around its edges onto a piece of cardboard (the back of a cereal box will do) to create an outline.

2. Drawing on one side of the cardboard, divide the outline into puzzle pieces. You can use traditional jigsaw shapes or just draw random intersecting lines to make unusual pieces instead.

3. With paper glue or double-sided tape, stick the picture to the other side of the cardboard and leave to dry, if necessary.

4. Cut carefully around your drawn lines using a craft knife or sharp scissors. This can be very finicky and you might have to alter your shapes at times, if they are too small to neatly cut. Trim off any ragged edges so that the pieces fit back together smoothly.

5. Mix up the pieces and enjoy your personalised jigsaw.

CLEAN UP YOUR ACT

ADVENTURERS	LOCATION	DIFFICULTY
👤	🚶	👍 👍 👍

Earn yourself a good citizen award by spending a spare hour picking up litter around your area. Of course, I know it's not your rubbish, but instead of wasting energy being annoyed, better to use it restoring the beauty of the landscape. Double your adventure up with a daytrip and head to a beach or woodland to tidy up instead. With just a few bin bags, some decent gloves and a strong stomach, you'll erase the damage of untidy humans and feel pretty smug about it too.

(I lied about the award, by the way.)

PERFECT FOR: improving community spirit, feeling better than your neighbours.

STUDY BUDDY

ADVENTURERS	LOCATION	DIFFICULTY
🧍	🏠 🚶	👍 👍 👍

Being a guinea pig doesn't have to mean eating hay and snuffling through the undergrowth. Taking part in research projects, online or in person, can be interesting, rewarding, and a great way to contribute to societal or medical progress.

PERFECT FOR: being part of something bigger than yourself.

Activities range from answering surveys to testing new products; you could even help count penguins in Antarctica from the warmth of your own home. Contact local universities for details on local opportunities to take part or look online for worldwide citizen science projects. Just remember, don't take part in anything you don't feel comfortable with and never disclose any personal information or banking details.

STRING TIME

ADVENTURERS	LOCATION	DIFFICULTY
🧍	🏠	👍 👍 👍

Raid your shed and make a rustic piece of string art to hang on your wall. You'll need a piece of wood, some thin nails or panel pins, a hammer, and string.

PERFECT FOR:
a noisy but strangely
relaxing afternoon.

How to:

1. Draw or print out your chosen design on paper and stick it to the wood. Simple shapes work best for this craft.

2. Hammer your nails about halfway through the pattern and into the wood, following the lines of your design and spacing evenly around 1 centimetre apart.

3. Rip off the paper and tie the end of your string to one of the pins. Move to your next pin and wrap your string around once, continue in the same way around your image. You can follow the outline first then fill in the inside, if you want to be methodical about it.

⚠PLEASE ADVENTURE RESPONSIBLY!

MORSE INSPECTOR

ADVENTURERS	LOCATION	DIFFICULTY
🧍	🏠	👍 👍 👍

On those days when you want to send a passive aggressive message to your noisy neighbours without having to face the consequences, learn Morse code and exorcise your anger through the wall and they'll never even know what you called

PERFECT FOR:
secret protests.

them. You can use a whistle, horn or torch to transmit the series of dots and dashes that make up the Morse code alphabet across a distance, but to chastise next door, just tap out your rant with long and short raps of your knuckles on the adjoining wall and feel your anger dissipate.

A ·– B –··· C –·–· D –·· E · F ··–· G ––· H ···· I ·· J ·––– K –·– L ·–·· M –– N –· O ––– P ·––· Q ––·– R ·–· S ··· T – U ··– V ···– W ·–– X –··– Y –·–– Z ––··

SHADY BUSINESS

ADVENTURERS	LOCATION	DIFFICULTY
🧍	🏠	👍 👍 👍

Shadow puppetry is a perfect lying on the couch, bored out of your mind activity, since your hands are all you need to try it – and they weren't busy anyway, right? Practise linking your thumbs together to make a basic butterfly or droop one hand down as a trunk

PERFECT FOR: entertaining yourself when you're bored of entertaining yourself.

and interlink your fingers around the trunk as tusks. When you've mastered the shapes, leave the sofa and find a torch or lamp to illuminate your hands and see if the shadows really do represent a convincing elephant or if you just look like a proper dumbo instead.

HANDMADE HELICOPTER

ADVENTURERS	LOCATION	DIFFICULTY
👤	🏠	👍 👍 👍

You have one sheet of paper, a paperclip and three minutes to create something interesting: what do you make? If you can't think of anything beyond a neat filing system, here's a quick project for you. Put together a paper helicopter that flies in a matter of moments then spend the rest of the time boasting about how excellent you are.

PERFECT FOR: screen-free entertainment.

How to:

1. Cut a rectangular strip of paper (around 20 × 5 centimetres) then fold it in half, bringing the two short ends together.

2. Open the fold back out and on one half, cut from the centre of the short end, stopping 1 centimetre from the fold. Fold your new rotors in opposite directions: one forward, one backward.

3. On the other half, make a cut on either long side, about 0.5 centimetre from the centre fold. Fold each side in towards the middle so that they overlap. Fold up a small piece at the bottom of this section and attach your paperclip here to keep it in place.

4. Throw your helicopter in the air and watch it spin.

TIME ON YOUR HANDS

ADVENTURERS	LOCATION	DIFFICULTY
🧍	🏠	👍 👍 👍

You'll have to make an early start for this one, but the result will transport you back in time. Make your own sundial and you'll never have to wear a watch again – at least when you're in the garden.

PERFECT FOR:
old school clock watching.

Find a small patch of grass that catches a lot of sun and push a straw or straight stick into the ground somewhere in the middle. On the hour, every hour during the day, place a marker (a stone will do fine) where the shadow of your stick falls. Keep going until the sun goes down then stand back and marvel at your primitive clock. Sadly, you will have to wait until morning to know the time again though.

BIRD OF PLAY

ADVENTURERS	LOCATION	DIFFICULTY
👤	🏠	👍 👍 👍

Prove you are the master of gravity with this balancing bird project. On a piece of card, draw an outline of a bird as though from the top down. Since the bird should be symmetrical, it's easier to fold your card and draw half of the bird on one side. The bird's wings should extend forward beyond its head and beak.

PERFECT FOR: a quick but entertaining project, pretending you understand science.

How to:

1. Cut out your bird and try to balance it by its beak on the end of your finger – probably unsuccessfully.

2. Attach a paperclip to the tip of each wing then try again. If it still doesn't work, move the paperclips up the wings, remembering to keep them in the same place on either side, until it does.

3. Spend hours marvelling at your genius.

STICK 'EM UP

ADVENTURERS	LOCATION	DIFFICULTY

Plants are a soothing addition to any home. But if, like me, you can't keep them alive for longer than it takes to get them back from the garden centre, best just to start with something pre-deceased and work with that instead. Pick up some branches from around the park, and turn them into stick weaving art that you can display in your vases after the flowers have long gone. Your sticks should be Y-shaped, in order to be made into small looms.

PERFECT FOR: bringing nature indoors.

How to:

1. Tie the end of some string or twine around one leg of the Y, close to the bottom juncture and zigzag it across the space between the two branches, wrapping it around several times on each turn to hold it in place. Secure with another knot at the top, making sure everything is taut.

2. Now you have your loom, you can start weaving. Using different colours of yarn or ribbon, wind over then under the strings of your loom, from the bottom to the top and back again. A darning needle can help to make this less fiddly, but isn't necessary if you don't have one to hand. You can start at either end or in the middle, building up the pattern as you go.

3. Change your colour at the bottom and you can tie off and cut your ends afterwards or leave them to dangle loose to add fringing to your design. Fill up the loom, bunching your yarns together throughout the process to ensure there are no gaps. Continue weaving until the loom is full. Make several in similar colour tones and display them together in a bunch or add a loop of string at the tip and turn them into pretty wall hangings.

DOLLED UP

ADVENTURERS	LOCATION	DIFFICULTY
👤	🏠	👍 👍 👍

PERFECT FOR:
all-age crafting.

Did you know that before plastic was invented, dolls were regularly constructed from yarn? I made that up but it's probably true, and yarn dolls are definitely a thing so I had to introduce this activity somehow. To try this traditional craft, you will, of course, need yarn – any colour or fibre content will do – and a piece of cardboard the same length as you want your doll to be.

How to:

1. Wrap the yarn around the cardboard as many times as you like. The more you wrap, the fuller your doll will be.

2. Slide the yarn off the cardboard carefully. Cut through one end of your circle of yarn to give you long strips of the same length.

3. Make your doll's head by twisting the middle of your strips together and tying a small section off at the top with another piece of yarn.

4. Separate the rest of your doll into three sections for the body and arms. Tie another piece of yarn around the middle of the body section then leave the bottom loose as a skirt or split into two legs.

5. Braid the arms and legs or wrap yarn around them then tie them at the ends.

6. Even off the bottom with scissors or don't bother and call your doll rustic instead.

FIRE IT UP

ADVENTURERS	LOCATION	DIFFICULTY
🧑 🧑	🏠	👍 👍

Wait, put down that 200-gram rocket and step away from the matches. For a fun, pretty and safe fireworks display at home, you have to make sure your sparklers are specifically for indoor use. If you haven't heard of indoor fireworks, prepare to be dazzled by their

PERFECT FOR: modest celebrations.

effects on a dull Tuesday evening. Boxes of assorted pyrotechnics for livening up rainy day get-togethers have been widely available since they were popularised in the seventies, and they make a joyful, if not quite Bonfire Night worthy, spectacle when you're not doing anything much else anyway.

Gather at a cautious distance around the kitchen table, lay out a heatproof plate or tray, and light up those strobes, fountains and sparklers to the oohs and aahs of your family. Add a few oohs and aahs of your own if you like, but not until you've ensured there's a basin of water on hand to keep the party as fire-retardant as possible.

⚠PLEASE ADVENTURE RESPONSIBLY!

INVISIBLE INK

ADVENTURERS	LOCATION	DIFFICULTY
👤 👤	🏠	👍 👍

Feel like a spy or a scout and send notes that no-one else can read. Dip a fine paintbrush or cotton bud in lemon juice, write your message on a blank sheet of paper and watch it disappear as it dries. To reveal your note, the recipient only has to heat up the letter by holding it over a lightbulb or candle or pressing it with a dry iron. Easy. All you have to do first is decide what classified material you want to pass on.

PERFECT FOR:
acting like an Enid Blyton character.

TREATS

Adventures, whether in far off lands or much closer to home, can be exciting and exhilarating and utterly exhausting. After a hard day of exploring then, it's important to leave a little bit of time to relax. Instead of just putting your feet up though, you can use this as another opportunity to try something new. Just remember that if you're not having fun, it's time to move on to the next page because treats don't have to be earned, but they do have to be enjoyed!

WINDOW SWAP

ADVENTURERS	LOCATION	DIFFICULTY
👤	🏠	👍

Look out of your window. What do you see? An awesome seascape or a suburban sprawl? No matter what your current view, it's always nice to have a change, and swapping your window is an easy way to see life from a different angle. There's already a

PERFECT FOR: travelling the world from your sitting room, brightening up a dull day.

thriving window swapping community online (just search for window swap to find the website), but for something a bit more personal, you can arrange your own trade with friends and family. Just send each other a photo (either digitally or in the post) or video of your favourite outlook from home, and display what you receive on your window ledge, desk or coffee table where you can glance at it regularly. Take a few moments throughout the day to imagine yourself in that space and enjoy a mental tour of the globe.

SECRET STREAKING

ADVENTURERS	LOCATION	DIFFICULTY
🧍	🏠	👍

Streaking isn't just for sports fans with high blood alcohol levels, and as long as it's done without an audience, your exposure doesn't have to be indecent. Next time you're home alone, close your curtains (very firmly, unless you want nosy neighbours seeing your every crook and nanny), and strip off. That's it, right off. Remember to turn the heating on beforehand, if it's winter, or put mittens on whatever you need to keep warm. Now run, walk or frolic through your house and giggle like crazy all the way. Do star jumps on the stairs or cartwheels in the conservatory. Go on, it's incredibly freeing, great for the soul and nobody ever has to know.

PERFECT FOR: days when you're feeling hot.

⚠ PLEASE ADVENTURE RESPONSIBLY!

POSTCARDS FROM HOME

ADVENTURERS	LOCATION	DIFFICULTY
🧍	🏠	👍

If you have ever taken joy in writing out postcards from seaside holidays, you'll probably be conjuring images of exotic stamps and scribbled notes in the sunshine. But you don't have to be sporting your best bathers to enjoy this quaint and gentle pleasure. The joy of diarising even the least eventful day and keeping in touch with friends and family in this charming way can be conjured just as easily from home.

PERFECT FOR: bringing holiday feelings home.

You can buy postcards from your local tourist shop or make one from a photograph backed with card. Use your favourite pen and try to distil your day down to the weather, food and quality of entertainment on offer. Add in a cheeky comment about your tan lines, if you must. And you can always wear your best swimwear to the post box, if you really want to.

DIGITAL DETOX

ADVENTURERS	LOCATION	DIFFICULTY
🧍	🏠🚶	👍

While turning off your devices sounds easy –
power buttons aren't poisonous – taking a
break from screens can be difficult. But
whether you can only manage an hour after
work or a full weekend without those backlit
beauties, you'll feel the benefit of giving your
brain a chance to reconnect with the environment around you,
when you allow it to disconnect from technology for a while.
Switch them all off and switch yourself on to the pleasures of
real life.

PERFECT FOR:
resting a busy
brain, feeling
like it's the
eighties.

FORTRESS OF SOLITUDE

ADVENTURERS	LOCATION	DIFFICULTY
👤	🏠	👍

There's no shame in wanting to hide from the world for a few hours. Spending time on your own in a comforting space can be restorative, and what better way to earn that rest than by building a burrow to enjoy it in. Pull together some pillows, sofa cushions, kitchen chairs and blankets, and erect your perfect den in the middle of your floor or a quiet corner of the bedroom. Lavish or basic, with or without structural integrity, your new hideout has only one purpose so snuggle in, hang a Do Not Disturb sign, and relax.

PERFECT FOR:
hiding, pretending you're five years old.

MAKE A SPLASH

ADVENTURERS	LOCATION	DIFFICULTY
🧑	🚶	👍

Hurrah, it's raining! Adventures don't have to stop because it's wet outside. In fact, one of the most joyful ways to spend a few minutes of any autumn day is having a good splash around. Puddles aren't just an annoying way to ruin a good suede shoe, they're a great resource for

PERFECT FOR: childish fun, giving your neighbours something to talk about.

showing us the brighter side of even the greyest clouds. Pull on some wellies, head outside and find the biggest puddle around. For a discreet wade, you can opt for a quiet street or just wander casually through any puddles that happen to be in your way. If you're feeling bold, skip merrily through the drizzle, kicking up some spray or go for full childhood fun, strip off your socks and allow yourself a barefoot splosh.

FREE HUGS

ADVENTURERS	LOCATION	DIFFICULTY

Sure, it takes a bit of courage to stand around the town centre with a FREE HUGS sign, but in these days of social distancing, or if physical contact with strangers just isn't for you, it's much more practical to try giving out virtual free hugs instead. Take a photo or record a video of your best hug then send it out to all those with whom you want to share it. It will warm your heart how many virtual hugs you receive in return – even if it doesn't quite warm your body.

PERFECT FOR: warming your cockles.

GENTLE EXERCISE

ADVENTURERS	LOCATION	DIFFICULTY
👤	🏠 🚶	👍 👍

Stop. Before you baulk at the suggestion that exercise can be a treat and throw the book across the room, focus on the gentle part and stick with me. We all know that moving our bodies a bit more is good for our health, and for some it's both a necessity and a passion. Take half an hour, whenever you can spare it, and focus on a little bit of movement, not to invigorate your body but to rest your mind.

PERFECT FOR: relieving tension, earning more cake.

Tai Chi
If you have ever spotted someone exercising in the local park moving their arms and legs gracefully, as though in slow motion, you have probably witnessed tai chi in action. This traditional Chinese martial art has become popular across the world for its health benefits and meditative qualities. Finding a local class is the best way to get started with the basics of tai chi, as it takes time and proper instruction to learn the right sequences and movements, but there are plenty of books and online tutorials to try, if you just want to check that it's right for you first.

Seated stretches

Sit right where you are and take a few deep breaths. Try to have your feet on the floor and wear warm clothes to help protect cold muscles from injury. Tilt your head slowly from side to side, rotate your wrists, wiggle your fingers and toes. Concentrate on your different muscle groups one at a time and move them smoothly and without force. Stretching is great for keeping bodies mobile and flexible. Just take it easy and appreciate each small sensation as you go.

Silent disco

Grab your headphones, stick on your favourite upbeat music and twirl around the house without anyone outside of your own ears knowing what is going on in there. Dancing is great to improve mood, whether you jiggle your entire being or quietly sway on the sofa. You don't even need music to enjoy a silent disco, just skip around to the tune in your head and lose yourself in the movement for a little while.

HOMEMADE STRESS BALL

ADVENTURERS	LOCATION	DIFFICULTY
👤	🏠	👍 👍

When you've had a demanding day and no amount of treats will lift the tension, you might just need something to take your frustration out on safely instead. With just a few supplies, you can make your own stress ball and squeeze it, throw it or just gently scold it until you feel better about life.

PERFECT FOR: channelling pent-up emotions, not punching people.

You will need a balloon, enough flour to fill it to a small ball size, and a plastic bottle.

How to:

1. Cut the top off the bottle to use it as a funnel, remove the cap and secure the opening of the balloon over the rim.

2. Stretch out the balloon or blow it up once or twice first to make it a little less stiff but take the air out before you introduce the flour, or you'll end up with nothing more than a cloud and a mess to clear up.

3. Fill the balloon with the flour until it's big enough to fit nicely into your hand. It helps to add small amounts of flour at a time and use the end of a spoon or pencil to pack it inside.

4. When you're happy with its size, remove your funnel and tie off the balloon's end.

5. Draw a jaunty face on the front, if you're in the mood, then thoroughly punish it for its irritating good cheer!

Tip: Consider making this as a craft project during a calm time in your life, before you are feeling stressed. Otherwise, by the time you've battled the flour into the balloon, cleaned up the overspill and found a pen that works, you might need this stress ball more than when you started.

GO IT ALONE

ADVENTURERS	LOCATION	DIFFICULTY
👤	🚶	👍 👍

Adventures can be great social experiences but, if you're always surrounded by people, it can be a real indulgence just to head out alone for an afternoon. Go to the cinema and see something you really fancy, take a walk and stop for an individual picnic, book a table for one at your favourite restaurant, and prove to yourself that you are the best company around.

PERFECT FOR: getting away from it all, building confidence.

If you are a regular lone soldier, try doing something different on your own instead. Pick an activity that you've always wanted to try but never been able to convince anyone to join you on, and go all by yourself.

MUDDY THE WATERS

ADVENTURERS	LOCATION	DIFFICULTY
🧍	🚶	👍 👍

With reported benefits for beauty – skin-deep and otherwise – mud baths aren't just for our porcine friends. Before you head out to the nearest farm and jump in the pen beside Piglet though, the right type of mud is essential if you want to feel any cleansing or anti-inflammatory advantages. Many spas offer the treatment but, for a quick and local version, you can buy Rhassoul mineral clay from health stores and enjoy the mud of Morocco in your own home. Simply add enough water to make a sludgy consistency and smear it over your face and body or throw some in your bath and enjoy a restful soak.

PERFECT FOR:
spoiling yourself,
spoiling your
bathroom tiles.

FOREST BATHING

ADVENTURERS	LOCATION	DIFFICULTY
🧍	🚶	👍 👍

Unless you want to drag your tub into the nearest woodland, please don't expect to be lathering up during this one. Far from requiring your best shower cap, forest bathing is a Japanese practice that encourages relaxation through being in nature and experiencing it as fully as possible. Give yourself a morning off, leave the trappings of the city behind and listen to the call of the wild.

PERFECT FOR: starting the day right, escaping the city.

There are lots of online resources for full instructions on forest bathing, but if you just want to give it a try, here are a few basics:

- Head into a forest or wood, away from other visitors so you won't be disturbed. Remember to tell someone where you are going first, for the sake of safety.

- Walk slowly, breathing in the scents of the trees.

- Engage all of your senses to connect with your surroundings. Touch the leaves and watch any wildlife.

- Take time to sit quietly, drinking in the colours and sounds of the area.

- Try not to worry if you're doing it right or not, just focus your mind on the wonders of nature around you and you'll feel the benefits anyway.

PLAY TIME

ADVENTURERS	LOCATION	DIFFICULTY
🧑	🚶	👍 👍

Who decided that we should all stop playing as soon as we start growing underarm hair? I don't know about you but I can't imagine it getting in the way on the seesaw. If you have ever passed a play park and longed for that youthful glee you once felt, push aside adult embarrassment and run straight in. Sure, some of the equipment might be a bit under-sized for your modern-day frame, but I promise you can never outgrow fun.

PERFECT FOR: boring weekdays, having more fun than your kids.

Don't be creepy: if there are kids around, leave them to it. But if you happen to spot an abandoned swing in your local area when schools are already in, don't just walk by. Jump on, feel the muscle memory kick in as your body tries to rock you higher and higher, and let yourself delight in the freedom of childhood play once more.

OFF SEASON

ADVENTURERS	LOCATION	DIFFICULTY
👤	🏠 🚶	👍 👍

The Gregorian calendar is so last year. With
its rigid schedule and tidy numbering system,
it just doesn't leave room for spontaneity.
Unless, of course, you ignore it completely
and pick your own dates to commemorate.
Christmas in summer, new week New Year,

PERFECT FOR:
celebrating every
day, an excuse to
leave the
tinsel up.

an extra birthday every few months: there's no reason to wait
until events come back around. If you feel like celebrating, just
pull out your favourite decorations and do it today. Or go one
step further and make up your own holiday altogether. I, for one,
have always thought the world lacks an International Fidgeting
Day.

FACIAL YOGA

ADVENTURERS	LOCATION	DIFFICULTY
🧍	🏠	👍 👍

The benefits of yoga for the body are well-known, but have you ever considered giving your face a more localised workout? Facial stretches are reportedly effective for strengthening muscles and relieving tension. They also lead to very silly expressions so, even if the wrinkles stick around, at least you'll have a few new laughter lines too.

PERFECT FOR: adding to your exercise routine without going near the gym.

Try these for starters:

Cheeks
Open your mouth wide, as though you're in the dentist's chair, then wrap your lips over your teeth. Now smile. Release and repeat this a few times more.

Forehead
Spread out your fingers on both hands and rest your fingertips on the middle of your forehead. Draw them out from the centre to your temples, putting light pressure into the movement. Spend 30 seconds doing this, slowly and without pulling at your skin.

Eyes
Let your jaw relax and place your hands on either side of your face, with your middle fingers at the end of your eyebrows. Apply gentle pressure and sweep your hands up towards the back of your head, holding the skin taut. Hold for a few seconds then start again.

WILD WINDOWS

ADVENTURERS	LOCATION	DIFFICULTY
🧍	🏠	👍 👍

You don't have to travel further than your
window to find nature worth capturing – and
using a camera instead of a net is much
more socially acceptable. Spending a few
hours watching local wildlife, picking your
moment, and taking the perfect photo can be
a contemplative and satisfying process, and you can even do it
in your pyjamas. Just be careful not to scare off your subjects.

PERFECT FOR:
a peaceful way to
start the morning.

GO SLOW DAY

ADVENTURERS	LOCATION	DIFFICULTY
🧑	🏠 🚶	👍 👍

When you feel overwhelmed, like life is too fast and busy, try slowing down the one thing you have control over – yourself. It sounds completely counterintuitive to apply the brakes when you already have too much to do and not enough time, but relaxing your pace and taking a more methodical approach helps to reduce stress and improve focus on individual tasks. By eliminating the time wasted on hurrying, you'll achieve more and feel less harried afterwards too.

PERFECT FOR: learning to value your time, hindering your entire household.

Be realistic: you can't pick the kids up an hour late and expect the school not to question your decision, but the washing up won't complain if it takes five minutes longer than usual, and you'll feel much calmer without all the rush.

FREE YOUR MIND

ADVENTURERS	LOCATION	DIFFICULTY
🧑	🏠 🚶	👍 👍

The obvious go-to activity for self-care is meditation but if, like me, you find it impossible to clear your head without bleach and a plunger, it can feel as though this mindful activity is not for you. Fortunately, not all meditation is the same so if you're struggling with the traditional process, try another technique instead:

PERFECT FOR: clearing a busy brain.

Guided meditation
When your thoughts are running wild and you can't find the path to enlightenment alone, having someone to tell you exactly what not to be thinking about is strangely useful. Go along to an in-person guided session locally or use one of the many online resources, apps or podcasts and let someone else do the work for you.

Active meditation

If you're unable to relax without having a project on the go, there are still plenty of ways you can spend your energy that will leave you feeling rested and fulfilled. By focusing your attention completely on a repetitive action, such as painting by numbers, running or even mowing the lawn, you can achieve a quiet, meditative state without having to sit cross-legged on a yoga mat.

FRIDGE SPA

ADVENTURERS	LOCATION	DIFFICULTY
🧍	🏠	👍 👍

Some days, a pamper session is all we really
want. But what if the shops are closed and
the health clubs just too pricey? Never fear,
throw on your fluffiest dressing gown, press
play on the Sounds of the Ocean playlist,
and head to the kitchen to brew up your own
DIY beauty spa from your leftovers instead. Remember to test
your products out on a little patch of skin first to make sure you
don't have any adverse reactions.

PERFECT FOR:
using up leftovers,
saving money on your
skincare regime.

Bath soak
For an easy, moisturising bath soak, just pick up a bowl of oats
and a blender. Blitz the oats into a powder then add them to your
bath water, giving it an instant antioxidant and anti-inflammatory
boost. Enjoy your relaxing bath for around 20 minutes then rinse
off any residue.

Exfoliating face mask

Breakfast isn't just the best meal of the day, it's the best for your skin too. Half a pot of natural yoghurt mixed with one or two teaspoons of ground coffee makes an excellent exfoliating mask. Apply it to your face and neck and leave for ten minutes then wash off with warm water and moisturise as normal.

Hair conditioner

Beer and eggs might make you think of a Friday night in a student flat, but they can do wonders for your hair, if not your aroma. Mix half a bottle of beer with a couple of eggs until smooth. Spread the mixture onto your hair and leave for 15 minutes. Rinse and admire your shiny locks.

HOBBY EXCHANGE

ADVENTURERS	LOCATION	DIFFICULTY
🧑 🧑	🏠 🚶	👍 👍

There's no better way to connect with another person than by showing interest in what's important to them, so prepare to bond with a hobby exchange. All you need for a hobby exchange is two or more people with a pastime to share and the time to pass sharing it. From pottery to pole dancing, you can trade with any fellow enthusiast, as long as both parties are willing and able to give the alternative activity a go.

PERFECT FOR: strengthening friendships, feeling like an expert.

Make up a mini beginners' course for your swap partner, send them your favourite books or tools, and congratulate them on their efforts with plenty of gold stars and praise. Take time to enjoy teaching someone what you love about your hobby and reignite your passion for it in the process. Not only might you gain another convert to your chosen pursuit, but maybe even a new-found interest of your own.

A hobby exchange lends itself really well to long-distance arrangements, so you don't even have to be in the same room – or country – to enjoy sharing recreation time with friends. And, if nothing else, this is a great excuse to indulge in your own favourite activity just that little bit more. Try your best to go into the project with an open mind; you might not fancy can-can dancing but remember that your friend gets a real kick out of it.

BOOK SNIFFING

ADVENTURERS	LOCATION	DIFFICULTY
👤	🏠	👍 👍

PERFECT FOR:
engaging your senses, being kicked out of the library.

Whether you love it or you don't, you can't deny it: books have their own distinctive aroma. For some, it adds to the experience of reading; for others, the smell of the pages prompts a hobby all of its own. Book sniffing is for anyone who has ever opened an old hardback and revelled in its comforting odour.

Next time the mood takes you, put your favourite novel to your nose, close your eyes and breathe it all in, noticing the different scents held within that cover. Simply take some time to enjoy any memories or images the smells conjure, or join fellow enthusiasts by jotting down your thoughts and observations in your own sniff notes. You are now officially a book sniffer. Congratulations, I think.

Not only does this sensory pursuit have an online club, it also has its own day: World Book Sniffing Day is celebrated on 12 December, but you don't have to wait until it comes back around to join in, since book sniffing is now an everyday pastime near all good bookcases across the world.

Go on, treat yourself, give me a sniff!

ABOUT THE AUTHOR

Paula 'Must Try Harder' McGuire is an adventurer, motivational speaker and life coach – but above all, she's a trier. After 30 years of surviving with chronic social anxiety and depression, Paula started to really live with it in 2012, using adventure as her means to recovery. She has since been a wing-walker, an athlete, a pilot, and even a trainee astronaut and spends what spare time she has encouraging others to turn barriers into climbing frames.

A double TEDx speaker, Paula regularly contributes to events around mental health and activity, and her first book – *Must Try Harder* – was published in 2018. She spent 2020 trying something new every day, from bridge-swinging to space-hopping and everything in between.

Paula lives in Scotland with her husband, Gerry, Agatha the dog, and Lionel the tortoise.